18.95

Arapahoe
13095
Westminst

MW00948850

Stems

Lynn Stone

Arapahoe Ridge LMC
13095 Pecos St.
Westminster, CO 80234

Rourke

Publishing LLC
Vero Beach, Florida 32964

© 2008 Rourke Publishing LLC

All rights reserved. No part of this book may be reproduced or utilized in any form or by any means, electronic or mechanical including photocopying, recording, or by any information storage and retrieval system without permission in writing from the publisher.

www.rourkepublishing.com

PHOTO CREDITS: All photos © Lynn Stone, except pg. 5 © ooyoo; pg. 6 © Ryan R McKenzie; pg. 7, 17 © Malcolm Romain; pg. 9 © Bruse Coleman; pg. 10 © Elena Elisseeva; pg. 12 © Lea Lysett; pg. 16 © Danny Smythe; pg. 18 © Alex Nikada; pg. 19 © Suprilono Sharjoto; pg. 20 © Bernd Lang; pg. 21 © Engin Communications

Editor: Robert Stengard-Olliges

Cover design by: Nicola Stratford, bdpublishing.com

Library of Congress Cataloging-in-Publication Data

Stone, Lynn M.
  Stems / Lynn Stone.
     p. cm. -- (Plant parts)
  ISBN 978-1-60044-556-9 (Hardcover)
  ISBN 978-1-60044-696-2 (Softcover)
  1. Stems (Botany)--Juvenile literature. I. Title.
  QK646.S76 2008
  581.4'95--dc22
                              2007015159

Printed in the USA

CG/CG

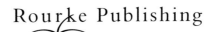

Rourke Publishing

www.rourkepublishing.com – rourke@rourkepublishing.com
Post Office Box 3328, Vero Beach, FL 32964

Table of Contents

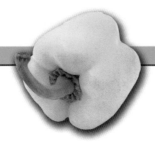

Plant Support

A plant stem helps support the flower and its upper parts. A stem also supports leaves. The stem helps leaves reach sunlight.

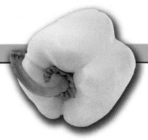

A plant stem has tubes inside it. The tubes allow water and plant food to move up and down. A stem works like a straw.

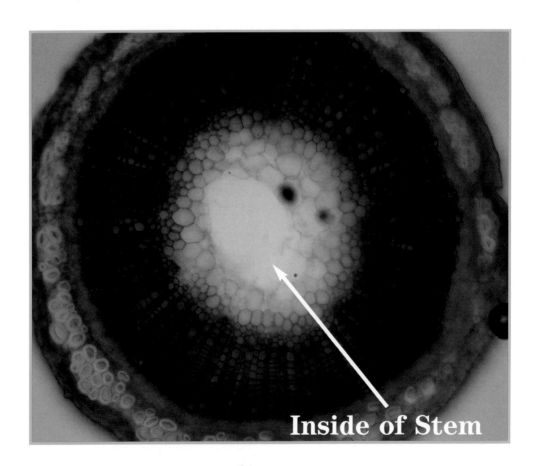

Inside of Stem

Water   Water

Leaves make food for plants. That food travels down the stem to the plant roots. Water and vitamins from soil move up the stem to the leaves.

Plant Food

Types of Stems

One type of stem is soft and green. It is known as a **herbaceous** stem.

Another type is the **woody** stem. Woody stems are hard. Tree trunks are the biggest woody stems. Tree branches are woody stems also.

Herbaceous Stem

Woody Stem

11

Most herbaceous stems die each year. Their roots may continue to live. Some of these roots make new stems each year.

Most garden flowers and vegetables have herbaceous stems.

13

Unusual Stems

Not all stems are like the stems of most flowers or trees. Cactuses are unusual stems. They are thick and **fleshy**.

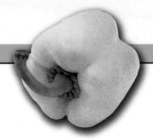

Another different type of stem is the **bulb**. Tulips, lilies, daffodils, and onions have bulbs.

Bulbs are plump underground stems. There are other types of underground stems, too.

Onion Bulb

Tulip Bulb

Underground Stems

Underground stems store food for plants. Stems are also food for people.

Farmers plant asparagus plants. The soft stems of young asparagus are table food.

Asparagus Stem

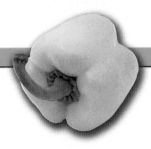

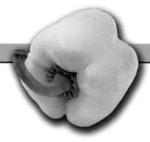

The part of the potato plant that we eat is an underground stem. This type of stem is called a **tuber**.

People also enjoy the celery stems we call "**stalks**."

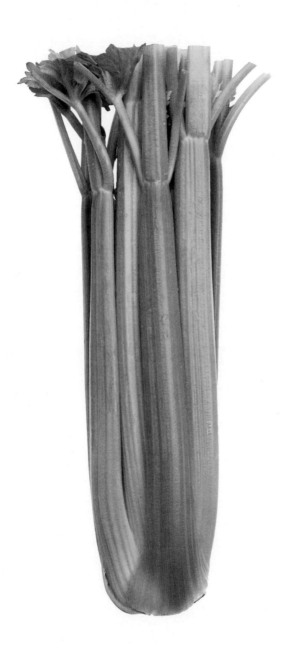

Glossary

bulb (BUHLB) — a type of ball shaped, underground stem

fleshy (FLESH ee) — soft and thick, like flesh

herbaceous (HUR ba shush) — plants or their parts that are soft and green

stalk (STAWK) — the long part of
a plant or the stem of a plant

tuber (TUBE er) — a type of thick
underground stem

woody (WOOD ee) — hard like
wood

Index

Further Reading

Bodach, Vijaya. *Stems*. Pebble Plus, 2007.

Farndon, John. *Stems*. Thomson Gale, 2006.

Websites to Visit

www.kathimitchell.com/plants.html

www.urbanext.uiuc.edu/gpe/case1/c1facts2a.html

www.picadome.fcps.net/lab/currl/plants/default.htm

About the Author

Lynn M. Stone is the author of more than 400 children's books. He is a talented natural history photographer as well. Lynn, a former teacher, travels worldwide to photograph wildlife in its natural habitat.